DISCOVERING
GOD'S
Grace

John Gillette's writings flow from a lifetime of experience. It is one thing to write out of a knowledge based on research. It is an entirely different thing to write out of a depth of life experience. John has both. As a pastor who has cared for the needs of a congregation, as a husband who has experienced the tragic loss of a wife, and as a child of God who has walked through the joys and pain of following the Lord, John has so much to offer in this series. From the opening pages, through to the very end, you will be blessed by the insights, loving tone, and encouragement you receive from this series. God has used John in ministry and will continue to use him through this life-giving series.

—*Josh Mateer, D. Min.*

True, illustrative, practical stories are like windows that unlock Bible truths and promises. Along with a masterfully orchestrated short stories should come the truth that God's Word and love has been experienced by His servants as they partner with Him in the work of rebuilding the Kingdom. A gifted teacher, Dr. Gillette lives an ordinary life abiding in Christ and being an obedient servant of the Lord. As he sees God working in his life, and in the lives of those to whom he ministers, his faith is refreshing, and he is encouraged to press on through life's uncertainties.

Only a lifetime dedicated to nurturing, ministering, teaching, and keen insight though the power of the Holy Spirit, can produce such poignant stories that teach and challenge.

—*Mulonge M. Kalumbula, Ph.D.*

John's books give us hope and light. He reminds us that through Jesus we are never alone. I have certainly needed that reminder in my life and in my practice. In holding a patient's hand, and helping them through a condition or disease, reminding them that they are never alone has become the greatest gift of health care.

—*Linda M. Kunce, D.C.*

The series reminds me that Jesus knows what it is like to live in a human body. I have received Jesus and His forgiveness, but as the book suggests, I also have the power from the Holy Spirit. His books have encouraged me to gain courage through prayer and confidence is Jesus to meet my needs. John's honesty is very special to read as he reflects on his own life and struggles. I like his explanation that "the soul is where the emotions are, and the mind is where the thinking takes place." It's been good for me to read that God works through weakness and learn that John found God with him in the middle of struggle.

—*Arvid W. Vandyke, Ed.D.*

Discovering God's counsel is a book full of great spiritual truths from someone who has developed a very close and deep relationship with Jesus through his life. John provides a meaningful and inspirational testimony, with examples from his own experiences, of how relying on God's Word and promises can give you the power, hope, and peace you need to overcome life's struggles and challenges. The Scriptures he chose in his book were on a point and helpful. It was an enjoyable and wonderful read.

—*Thoa Reyna, J.D.*

John has written a user-friendly and practical series for anyone desiring to live beyond the superficial and venture into the supernatural. The world needs this *Pastoral Health Care* series. Pastors and followers of Jesus need the insights from John's lifetime experience of walking with God and caring for His people through the power of the Holy Spirit. John has brilliantly show that God is enough, God's counsel is enduring, and God reigns supremely. This important series will serve both the church and the world for many years to come.

—*Kizombo Kalumbula, Jr., Ph.D.*

John Gillette's inspirational book *Glorify God* is a fantastic reminder of how I should approach each day and how blessed I am. It is so easy to get caught up in the hustle and bustle of today's lifestyle and forget what is really important. John's encouraging words are a great reminder of how we all should live each day. I have a great foundation of faith, but John's book helps me to remember what is important and allows me to reflect on the wonderful things I have and to be gracious to God for those blessings.

— *Tammy Thelen, Au.D., CCC-A*

John's book contains a lifetime of experiences guided by the law of the Bible, which reaches an important spiritual conclusion. This book is written to open your mind and self– consciousness to the Holy Spirit, which in turn provides a path to salvation. The book draws the reader closer to personal observation which provides reasoning to exact reference to scripture. Highly recommended for self-development of Christian faith."

—*Nicholas A. Reyna, Esq.*

FANTASTIC
FAVORITES
PART 2

DISCOVERING

GOD'S

Grace

*What does it mean to
magnify Jesus Christ?*

JOHN F. GILLETTE

Chapbook Press

Schuler Books

2660 28th Street SE

Grand Rapids MI 49512

www.schulerbooks.com/chapbook-press

Fantastic Favorites Book Series Part Two

Discovering God's Grace: What does it mean to magnify Jesus Christ?

Copyright ©2023 — John F. Gillette. All rights reserved. Published 2023.

Printed at Schuler Books, Chapbook Press, Grand Rapids, Michigan, in the United States of America.

Distribution contact:at jjgillette@comcast.net.

ISBN 13: 9781957169644

Library of Congress Control Number: 2023920879

Cover photo: Paige Weber/Unsplash
Cover Design: Frank Gutbrod Graphic Design

Printed in the United States of America

Books by John Gillette:

Pastoral Health Care

Discovering God's Sufficiency

Going Beyond Ourselves and Experiencing the Supernatural

Part One

Discovering God's Love

Confirming God's Love Through the Evidence of Historical Facts

Part Two

Discovering God's Counsel

Applying His Spiritual Solution to Meet Difficult Trials

Part Three

Discovering God's Kingdom

Finding a Way to Understand Ourselves in a Complex World

Part Four

Discovering God's Heart

Finding God's Heart Pulse is Our Daily Challenge

Part Five

Divine Dialogue

Glorify God

Christianity is a Divine Vitality

Part One

Dynamic Doer

Biblical Christianity is Jesus Christ

Part Two

Satisfying Strength

Biblical Meditation Works — Allow Psalms to Sweep You into All Directions

Part Three

Disciplining Dynamics

Christian Counseling Teaching Tools

Part Four

Celebrate Christ

Above All Christ

Part Five

Fantastic Favorites

Discovering God's Presence

What does it mean to live in Jesus Christ?

Part One

Discovering God's Grace

What does it mean to magnify Jesus Christ?

Part Two

Discovering God's Supernatural Activities

Why Do I Believe in Jesus Christ?

Part Three

Discovering God's Eternal Life

What have I learned about Jesus Christ?

Part Four

Discovering God's Church

How did Jesus Christ's church begin?

Part Five

Joy and John Gillette

It is with great affection that I dedicate this book series to my wife Joy, who radiated God's grace. We wrote the Pastoral Healthcare Series together. Applying God's spiritual solutions to meet us in difficult trials has become even more practical in my life with the recent death of my dear wife, Joy.

This book has been reproduced in her memory while the content is the same, my dedication has become more personal than ever before. The separation is painful, but as I gather my suffering and feelings of incompleteness, I will succeed with God's peace and presence. The guidelines of this book have brought blessing to our life together. We have pursued them with great persistence. I am assured she is in God's presence rejoicing and at peace. I will be with her to experience God's eternal presence someday as well. " . . . Blessed are they who put their trust in him." (Psalm 2:12)

I appreciate all the people that God has used to influence me. Many of these thoughts have come to my memory over the past eighty-three years through sermon notes, lectures, conversations, meditations, and readings. I have not knowingly withheld any significant reference from others in my devotional. To the best of my knowledge, all statements and information are true and correct and given credit. Everyone I have come in contact with should be given credit. The devotional is a constant source of strength, support, and security for me, and I hope also for you.

Table of Contents

Wonderful Grace of Jesus

2 Corinthians 8:9

The songwriter has written "Wonderful grace of Jesus, greater than all my sin. How shall my tongue describe it? Where shall its praise begin? Taking away my burden, setting my spirit free; for the wonderful grace of Jesus reaches me." *Discovering God's Favor* is my spiritual autobiography. It is the life of a triplet, a triplet that was born with a triple desire to serve God through music, ministry and mentoring. He was driven by passion, independence and diversity. It uses key hymns and spiritual song phrases to introduce each chapter's theme. It follows with a devotional scripture. Biographical illustrations will show how the Biblical truth may mold life. God is working. Is he working in your life? Look at your life closely and you may be surprised and be drawn closer to him. Through reading my testimony, the hope is that you will know God better.

I have been blessed with a deep desire and have been given reliable resources to push me forward. Some people have a problem with a lack of interest in what I am writing about. Some people will diligently search for an answer and remain perplexed with all the hindrances of the day. Some people are led down the wrong path by religious fanatics. Some people are just plain blind to the truth.

I have been blessed with having parents who have been led in the belief that Jesus Christ is Savior and Lord. They have pursued every means to instruct me in the way, the truth and the life. As a matter of fact, the thing I remember most is that my grandmother would sit in her rocking chair, praying and reading her Bible. My parents continued the journey discipling me in such a way that my heroes would be preachers, evangelists and missionaries. Today, I listen to their sermons and I can remember their faces and platform deportment.

I have been blessed to rely upon a belief system that is in a person who is God. Biblical authority has not been doubted because when I mix the Word with faith, it works. This absolute truth has become a solid rock for me. I have studied it, have taught it, have tested it, and have looked at the haters of the truth, the ignorant of the truth, the scholars and even believers that have a problem with it during difficult times in their lives. I have been blessed to be secure in my doctrinal beliefs in Jesus Christ They have been sound from the beginning. What I believed in my childhood, I believe now in my senior years.

Belief in God has become steadfast in my life because I have grown in his grace. I know a lot of people that are not secure and I think they have to let go of self. The trinity of self - me, myself and I - are getting in the way. I have been blessed to live with the inner courage to follow Jesus. The Holy Spirit indwells me. He is my witness that God the Father has chosen me, God the Son has purchased me and God the Holy Spirit has sealed me. The more I pursue him, the more I realize that he is pursuing me. The holy urge is always prompting me as I allow the Holy Scriptures to penetrate my soul. I have been blessed with his benefits. Christianity is practical and it gives me a life that is abundant and overflowing. Even during unrest, worry, confusion and confrontation, God makes his presence felt. I know he is near because I am living in the moment with him. The Bible says, "God is able to make all grace abound to you so that in all things at all times, having all that you need, you will abound in every good work" (2 Corinthians 9:8). *Discovering God's Favor* is filled with God's graciousness. Grace is what God does for me, not what I do for God or for myself. Salvation is God's greatest gift and my greatest need. God gives and I receive. Grace is God's channel for me to receive God's free gift (Hebrews 11:6). Faith is the means for me to experience grace. I am his 'workmanship' (Ephesians 2:10). Christ is for me (grace); it is Christ in me (faith) and Christ through me (works). I will 'abound' because God is working through his grace. When the kingdom of God is placed first, the temporal needs are included. I have to practice righteousness. How do I do that? ..by constant seeking. This means that my dominant concern is spiritual, not material. It means I have a continued hunger and thirst after righteousness. It is setting my affection on things above. It is seeking holiness. It is the desire to know God better.

The priority is to 'think correctly'. To 'think correctly' means to think biblically. I have encircled my life with these thoughts concerning grace. "And the word became flesh and dwelt among us, and we saw his glory, glory as of the only begotten from the Father full of grace and truth" (John 1:14). In the Scripture there are numerous demonstrations of grace. It is to "extend favor or kindness to one who doesn't deserve it and can never earn it." God came to earth through the goodness of his heart to "stoop down" and give us a forgiveness and acceptance into his kingdom. As I travel through my spiritual autobiography, it is

God who provides salvation and has chosen me to live a holy life. He did this not because I deserved it but because that was his plan long before the world began – to show his love and kindness to me through Christ Jesus (2 Timothy 1:9). I have been eternally justified on the basis of grace. It is a gift and is absolutely free. I cannot boast. It is by grace through faith (Ephesians 2:1-9). As I travel through my spiritual autobiography, it is God that provides peace (Romans 5:1).

My sovereign God declares me righteous even while I am in a sinning state. That transaction begins a process of growth toward maturity. It is progressive. Day by day, I learn to honor Christ. I am grateful to God for repentance, forgiveness, belief, justification, justice and grace. As I travel through my spiritual autobiography, it is God that provides my needs. "For the Lord God is a sun and shield; the Lord gives grace and glory. No good thing does he withhold from those who walk uprightly" (Psalm 84:11). His grace is observed through each chapter. The "Wonderful Grace of Jesus" provides: Victory, Belief, Love,

Focus, Redemption, Transformation, Faith, Renewal, Guidance, Fellowship, Trust, Success, Order, Dependence, Desire, Silence, Relationship, Submission, Peace, Reliance, Blessings, Intimacy, Comfort, Enablement, Glory, Hope, Communion, Intervention, Service, Confidence, Security, Submission, and Peace.

As I travel through my faith journey, it is God that provides undeserved and yet unconditional love. "But by the grace of God I am what I am, and his grace toward me did not prove vain" (1 Corinthians 15:10). I am not interested in this world's ego-centered kingdom but rather the kingdom of heaven (Matthew 6:33). I challenge you to write your own spiritual autobiography. Share your own personalized statement regarding how God's grace affects your life. I hope I can, along with the New Testament writers, mention the grace of God in both my greetings and my closing remarks. I have been blessed by his grace, that "Wonderful Grace of Jesus." Join me on my life's journey!

Onward Christian Soldiers
Ephesians 6:10-20

The songwriter has written, "Onward Christian Soldiers! Marching as to war, with the cross of Jesus going on before. Christ, the royal master leads against the foe." As a teenager and young adult, this song was a favorite. It was a fantastic trumpet solo. You can imagine the soldiers marching. The single, triple and gruppetto tonguing would take you into victory. I played it many times to praise the Lord, and every time I was challenged to "stand up for Jesus" and go forward into battle. The low tones brought a solid foundation and the piercing high tones would scream out to get your attention.

I have begun with "forward into battle, with Christ's promises which can never fail" because my life can be traced through history with wars. Matthew 24:6-7 says "and ye shall hear of wars and rumors of wars: see that ye be not troubled: for all these things must come to pass but the end is not yet. For nations shall rise against nations…" I'm glad that Jesus Christ has been my family's "light and salvation, whom shall I fear?" "He shall hide me in His pavilion" (Ps. 27:1, 3-5).

My birth took place when World War II started. On August 31, 1939, Hitler and the Nazis staged a Polish attack on a minor German radio station in order to justify a German invasion of Poland. On September 1, Hitler declared war on Poland, and France and Britain had a defense pact with Poland. This forced France and Britain to declare war on Germany which they did on September 3. The Soviet Union invaded Poland from the east on September 17. The war in Europe was under full swing. The war in the Pacific was plotted by Japan and an Imperial takeover of Asia was underway. I was born along with my sisters on December 17, 1939. *The Grand Rapids Press* and *The Herald* newspapers would carry news of the war. At the same time for several years, the papers would also carry highlights of "the Christmas babies - triplets born." Birth is always a miracle. In my case, it was unique, amazing and God-touched. My parents didn't expect triplets. Their first baby weighed the same amount as the trio did. They were born at home due to the winter storm that caused everything to stop but birth. We were born in an upstairs apartment. Our first bassinette was a chest of drawers. Milk was provided because of publicity we had in the newspapers. We were the only set of triplets born in our birth year. We are one of the oldest set recorded in the official records in our county.

The act of creation is amazing. "And the Lord God formed man of the dust of the ground, and breathed into his nostrils the breath of life; and man became a living soul" (Genesis 2:7). This verse reveals to us that the body was made of the dust of the ground, that the spirit came from the breath of God, and that the combination produced the soul. Man is a soul; therefore, he has his own identity. The soul is self-conscientiousness. His personality is discovered through his intellect, emotion and will. His body is where the soul and spirit live. It is wonderfully made and has a story of its own to tell. The breath of God produced life and is the very nucleus of life. The Bible says, "For the Word of God is living and active, sharper than any two-edged sword. It penetrates even to the dividing of soul and spirit, joints and marrow, and it judges the thoughts and attitudes of the heart" (Hebrews 4:12 NIV).

In my childhood years, we would feel the effects of the Korean War occurring June 25, 1950 and a cease fire on July 27, 1953. This was a civil war between states of North Korea and South Korea that were created out of World War II. The principle support on the side of the North Korean communists was the People's Republic of China. The United Nations forces, primarily from the United States, supported South Korea. There was never a "real" end of the war. The conflict still technically persists to this day. It's hard to believe that at ten years of age, while pulling my red wagon down the street to a friend's house to play, that many casualties would be added to a list from a war dubbed the *Forgotten War* or the *Unknown War*. The United States would experience 33,685 battle deaths, 2,830 non-battle deaths, and 17,730 deaths of personnel outside the Korean theatre. There were also 8,142 United States personnel listed as *Missing in Action* during the war. This wouldn't account for the thousands from the enemy or other countries killed in action. The Korean War was the first armed confrontation of the Cold War and set the standard for many later conflicts. It created the idea of a limited war where the two superpowers would fight in another country making the people in that nation suffer the bulk of the destruction and death involved in the war between such large nations. The superpowers avoided descending into an all-out war with one another as well as the mutual use of nuclear weapons.

As I grew up into my teens and early twenties, the Berlin Wall surrounding West Berlin was built. More tension began to build. The Soviet Union had missiles that would be launched against Europe but U.S. missiles were capable of striking the entire Soviet Union. Cuba was only ninety miles off the coast of Florida. In April 1962, the Soviet Union conceived the idea of placing intermediate-range missiles in Cuba. The Cuban Missile Crisis was the closest the world ever came to a nuclear war. This was a scary time as I had just graduated from college with a degree in Theology (BTh). The draft was on my door step. I consulted about the possibility of auditioning for one of the military bands or completing my studies and joining the service as a Chaplain. Tension finally began to ease when the Soviet Union announced to dismantle missile installations and the United States agreed not to invade Cuba.

You would think, hopefully, that peace would be around the corner. Let's get on with the life goals and pursue happiness, but no such luck. Vietnam problems would create issues that demanded some answers. The communist north and the democratic south were in a battle for reunification. Three United States Presidents became involved with this war. One

President chose a middle route to follow, which was a limited partnership with South Vietnam. The second President chose to follow a plan of military intervention and sent combat troops. The third President would expand the war into Laos and Cambodia. A peace accord would be signed to end hostilities between the United States and Democratic Republic of Vietnam. The Paris Peace Agreement did not end the conflict in Vietnam. The communist forces captured Saigon. A promise to not abandon South Vietnam was agreed upon if certain peace accords would be signed. The promise was never kept.

The 60's and 70's were years of confusion, unrest, alternative thinking, turmoil, situation ethics, and less than a little genuine spiritual interest from a Biblical point of view. During those years I began pursuing a lifelong learning journey. I have never become studious for money, fame, prestige or any other reasons like that. I would study because I wanted to know more and be able to be more competent in what I happened to be doing at the time. I was always ready to learn new things and to keep my passionate, independent and diversified style of life. The studies would differ according to my interest which was pastoral, educational and para church leadership. Those years brought many possibilities in education. I always tried to balance the traditional with the alternative and the distance learning with the classroom. I wrote my own curriculum and I would sit under knowledgeable scholars. The years were exciting and adventurous. They laid the foundation for a future doctorate in Philosophy (PhD.), Biblical Christianity and a doctorate in ministries (DMin) with organizational development.

After World War II, the Korean War, Cuban Crisis and the Vietnam War, we would be faced with trouble in the Middle East and always trouble-conflict-unresolved issues in the East. In my adulthood, the Persian Gulf War would be on every television set. The power and speed to save little Kuwait would take place and even now the Iraq War that continues endlessly. Is World

War III around the corner? We live in days of war. The invisible war is everywhere. Against the body, Satan brings the temptations of the flesh. Against the soul, he brings the temptations of the world. Against the spirit, he chooses to come himself or sends one of his lesser agents. Attacks will be made and conflicts will continue.

It all started when Satan and sin entered the universe. God created the earth and the heavens with His word. Lucifer-Satan announced that he had to take possession of them for himself. By the simple word of God, the heavens and the earth toppled into judgment. In that same moment, Satan got his first mouthful of dirt. Dust in the mouth is a perfect figure for defeat and destruction. Satan had lifted himself toward heaven in a surge of awful desire to be like God, and his mouth was filled with dust. Every man or woman who wishes to be independent of God in Christ is in the path of Lucifer-Satan. Satisfaction is not to be found outside of God as he is revealed in Jesus Christ, with obedience to his will.

We can have victory in our war. We are able to abstain from temptation to the flesh (body). We are to believe and not conform to the world (soul). We are to resist Satan (spirit). The key words are flight, faith and fight. In my senior years, I'm learning to be a soldier that is marching with the cross of Jesus. I will conquer and be victorious as I daily put on God's armor. I would start every instrumental solo with scripture. With "Onward Christian Soldiers" I would use Ephesians 6:10: "My brothers, be strong in the Lord and in the power of his might." The power is found in the three words that represent Christ: 1) His death – strong, 2) His resurrection – power, and 3) His ascension - might. The trio would produce Pentecostal power. We can't fail when we allow this to work in our lives. If we want to stand, we must "Put on the whole armor of God" (Ephesians 6:11). We have an invisible conflict. It is a spiritual battle with the "Prince of the power of the air" (Ephesians 2:2). The strategy is to live life with integrity, purity, victory, security and the Word. The foundation is truth. It will hold everything together. Satan is a liar (John 8:44) and Jesus is the truth (John14:6). With integrity, we will have a clear conscience.

Our righteousness is received through Jesus (2 Cor. 5:21). The accuser, Satan, is a specialist in deception. Bad behavior breeds open opportunity for Satan. Our conduct must not give him any space. We must always have an attitude of repentance, confession, forgiveness and renewal. Our focus should always be on victory. Satan creates doubt and confusion but Jesus is our peace (Ephesians 2:14). We must march toward victory. We have divine support. He provides it right at the moment we need it. Faith is our shield. It will quench all the fiery darts of the wicked. Satan will try us with all sorts of things but Jesus gives us faith (Galatians 2:20). Keep in mind, "but ye are not in the flesh but in the spirit, if so be that the Spirit of God dwell in you…" (Romans 8:9-10). We are secure in him. He is doing the battle for us.

As we become rooted, built up and established in faith that Jesus provides us with, we will conquer. Satan likes to play tricks with our minds, but we are complete in Jesus when our mind stays focused. Salvation in Christ Jesus is our confidence and security. Jesus used the Scripture against the enemy "as it is written" (Luke 4:1-13), we are able to do the same. Keep marching forward as Christian soldiers.

Personal Response

Add your own review

1. What is the solid foundation?
2. Who is our enemy?
3. What does Ephesians 6:10 do for you?
4. What does victory mean to you (Eph. 2:14)?

Only Trust Him

Matthew 11:28-30

The songwriter has written, "Come every soul by sin oppressed, there's mercy with the Lord; and he shall surely give you rest by trusting in His Word. Only Trust Him, Only Trust Him, He will save you." He will give you rest. Have you read Jesus' words, "Come unto me" in Matthew 11:28-30? Have you heard His sweet, deep, sensitive, authentic, bold, eternal, and changing words?

"Come unto me" is an open invitation. Let's discover what Jesus means with such awesome words. We better start with a little background. The Gospel according to Matthew gives a view of the life of Jesus. Most likely, the early accounts were passed on verbally in the Aramaic language and then recorded in Greek manuscripts dating from A.D. 60 to A.D. 90. Matthew emphases the Old Testament preparation for the gospel and makes it an ideal "bridge" from the Old to the New Testament. Matthew, the Hebrew tax collector, writes for the Hebrew mind. He tells us that Jesus is the Messiah foretold by Old Testament prophets. He starts with the genealogy of Jesus. The coming of Christ to the earth has been anticipated from the beginning. In the early days of human history, God chose one family line, that of Abraham, and later on another family with the Abrahamic family, that of David, to be the family through which His son would make entrance into the world.

Miracles, lessons learned and many activities have already taken place, but now we have come to chapter eleven of Matthew, verses 28-30, to think about Jesus' sweet words "Come unto me." The purpose of the gospel is to present the good news of the Redeemer-Savior. Jesus is the Messiah of Israel, the Son of God, and the Savior of the World.

"Come unto me" are life-changing words but they can't be heard by our sinful, rebellious and stubborn minds without a sovereignly bestowed spiritual awakening. We read of a free offer to all in verses 28-30 and a divine initiative in verse 27. I'm so glad that the Holy Spirit convicts us and the sovereign work of God is at hand so that we can trust our spirit, soul and body to Jesus Christ. Authority and confidence are found in verse 27. "All things are delivered unto me of my father: and no man knoweth the Son, but the Father: neither knoweth any man the Father, save the Son, and he to whom so ever the Son will reveal Him." Jesus is the way initiated by the Father. "My Father" reveals Jesus' absolute equality; He is the "only begotten Son." Personal knowledge of the Father through the Son with the assistance of the Holy Spirit will develop assurance and authority in living. How does genuine conversion take place? The songwriter says, "Only Trust Him" and the text continues with the answer.

"All ye that labor and are heavy laden" are words that describe our condition. If we are going to hear God's call through Jesus, we have to be in a condition of humility. The labor and burden has brought us to exhaustion and just plain sweat. We have to lay our load at Jesus' feet. Trying to save ourselves will not work, doing all the good works will not do it, a guilty conscience will not do it, but a broken heart realizing total dependence is necessary. We will hear his voice "Come unto me" when we recognize our sinful condition. In the present condition we don't measure up to God's standards. In my childhood, I responded to Jesus. I had been singing with my sisters at a Bible Conference. On the way home, our mother asked if we would like to ask Jesus into our hearts. We knew the gospel story. Because of sin, we were separated from God (Romans 3:23), and the penalty for sin is death (Romans 6:23). Thankfully that penalty for sin was paid by Jesus Christ (Romans 5:8). If we repent of the sin (acknowledge need), then confess and trust Jesus as Lord and Savior (accept Jesus), we will be saved (Romans 10:9). Right there in the car by the side of the road, I was "born of God" and a second birth (spiritual) took place (I John 5:11-12). This birth is clearly stated in John 3:8, "The wind bloweth where it listeth, and thou hearest the sound thereof, but cannot tell whence it cometh, and whither it goeth: so is everyone that is born of the Spirit." The wind, which is the same word used for Spirit, cannot be seen or explained. The word can only be heard or observed in relation to its effect. The new birth is spiritual and invisible. One can only observe the results. It's a decision of faith based upon facts. The first element in trusting Jesus is total dependency.

"And I will give you rest… ye shall find rest unto your souls" are powerful words. It's not only a dependent heart that is necessary but the discovery of divine truth found in Jesus Christ who provides the rest for our souls. Liberation is given through Jesus. We can entrust our spirit, soul and body to Jesus because of who He is. In the Gospel of John, Jesus is revealed as the eternal, pre-existing Son of God, who became man in order to reveal the Father and bring eternal life through his death and resurrection. John says: "Now Jesus did many other signs in the presence of His disciples, which are not written in this book; but these are written that you may believe that Jesus is the Christ, the Son of God, and that believing you may have life in His name" (John 20:30-31).

Jesus is God. "In the beginning was the Word, and the Word was with God, and the Word was God. He was in the beginning with God." In John 1:14 it says that "the Word became flesh." The key term, Word, refers to Jesus. Jesus is fully God. These phrases are vital to understand. "In the beginning" refers to eternity past. It goes beyond his earthly life, beyond even the beginning of creation into eternity. "With God" refers to an affirmation of Christ's separate personality. There is diversity within the Godhead. "And God was the Word" refers to the fact that Jesus is fully divine in all respects. We can trust Jesus because He is God. He has the authority and power to redeem us and bring us into his family.

"Take my yoke upon you and learn of me; for I am meek and lowly in heart" are words of challenge and life-changing possibilities. We must turn around in our thinking. We must turn to Jesus and repent. Our way to acceptance and forgiveness is not acceptable. A complete turnaround and a full change of direction are necessary. We have come to the end of our resources. As we learn of Him, we discover our self-regulations. Work-based convictions will not be sufficient. He is gentle and tender and is calling us to Himself. As we turn from our sin and replace it with faith, a new direction takes place. This is not an intellectual exercise but a whole heart change.

"For my yoke is easy and my burden is light" are words that remind us that salvation in Jesus Christ includes an invitation to surrender. If we want His saving rest, we must take His yoke. The yoke is a symbol of submission. It is used by the master to direct us. Discipline is a natural result of all the elements that are a part of genuine conversion. The yoke is submission to Christ and is not grievous. It is joyous.

My childhood song to live by tells it all, "I have been chosen by the Father, purchased by the

Son, and sealed by the Spirit, I'm His Very Own" (Ephesians 1). As a child, I did not understand everything and I do not even now. His grace is amazing and His sovereignty is above us. All He wants me to do is take him at His word. He said, "By one man (Adam), sin entered into the world and death by sin, and so death passed upon all men for all have sinned" (Romans 5:12). "Behold I was shaped in iniquity" (Psalm 51:5). I do not like reading these words but God said it and I have to accept it. I have discovered that "Ye have chosen me" (John 15:16). "It is God who worketh in you both to will and to do of His good pleasure" (Philippians 2:13). He is drawing me to Himself (John 6:44). He has saved me and called me according to His own purpose and grace (II Timothy 1:9).

I am so glad that I was taught by my parents in the early years that "God commendeth His love toward us in that, while we were yet sinners, Christ died for us" (Romans 5:8). As I have grown in Jesus Christ, I have seen His sovereign grace at work. He saved me not by works of righteousness that I have done but according to His mercy by the working of regeneration and renewing of the Holy Spirit (Titus 3:5). I live every day knowing in whom I have believed and am persuaded that He is able to keep that which I have committed unto Him against that day (II Timothy 1:12). Salvation is of the Lord. I am safe because the Father has chosen me, the Son has purchased me and the Holy Spirit has sealed me. Salvation occurs when God changes the heart and unbelievers turn from sin to Christ (Colossians 1:13). Faith is the process for Jesus to enter the heart and dwell there (Ephesians 3:17). Praise the Lord!

Personal Response

Add your own review

1. What does the words chosen purchased & seal mean?
2. How do you practice faith?

Great is Thy Faithfulness
Psalm 23:1-6

The songwriter has written "Great is Thy Faithfulness, O God, my Father; there is no shadow of turning with Thee. Thou changest not; Thy compassions they fail not. As Thou has been Thou forever wilt be." In my childhood, I began singing praises to Jesus Christ. The Bible says in Psalms 57:911 "I will praise you, O Lord, among the nations; I will sing of you among the people. For great is your love, reaching to the heavens; your faithfulness reaches to the skies. Be exalted, O God, above the heavens; let your glory be over all the earth."

There was a real need to add space to our home. The new addition was built as one big room. It had a big window overlooking the front yard. In those days it seemed to be a large room. It was called our family music room. You could tell why in one glance. You would see a piano, marimba, vibraharp, trumpet, trombone and others. It became our play room and rehearsal space.

During our elementary years, the newspapers would pick up the information about the "triplets" performing. We were the first set of triplets ever to attend Palmer Grade School. It was an attention-getter: "Triple Time Threesome" will play at school carnival. In the Sunday Press, you might read "Triplets sing at Sunday Service." Both of our parents and older sister were active musicians. They were always ready to provide specials for just about any activity if it would glorify our Lord and Savior Jesus Christ.

As a little child, I found a tract entitled "The Lord is My Shepherd" based on Psalms 23:1-6. It became my first sermon, shared with animals and people. This Psalm has become a picture of my first ten years of living. My life has been rooted in God's great faithfulness. Without Psalm 22, there would be no Psalm 23. He who doesn't believe that Christ died for our sins has no claim on the comfort of the risen Savior. In the previous chapter, I shared how and when I made a confession of faith (Romans 10:9,10), "He came to seek and save that which were lost" (Isa.53:6). By accepting Jesus, he produced power and authority in my life. The relationship that was started in those days has continued through the years. I learned to let God be God in my thinking. Today I have to go back to my childhood thinking. As adults we try to fit him into our narrow small view. We must let him lead. He will meet every need. He is "Lord" and Master. He is my Shepherd, boss and caregiver. Music has provided the means for me to fulfill my passion of proclaiming His Word.

Those early years had some uncertainties in them. The World War was in process and the unexpected birth of three babies instead of one baby brought questions like how will God's unlimited resources provide our ever-increasing needs? When you work together and rely on God's promise "I shall not want," you are able to see things happen. Grandpa helped with the numerous diapers that needed washing and grandma helped with feeding the babies along with sister, Mary Lee. She was only three years older but was smart and quite able to help mother. Mother would do what mothers do and dad would spend many hard working hours to provide for us. If you would have asked them about it all, they would have said it was worth it all. They had received from God a special unexpected gift - triplets. God's love can never be diminished. He comes and watches over us. We learned in our childhood that "faith" should say, "I cannot want." He is almighty, all wise, all loving and never changing.

We made it through the birth years but both of my triplet sisters had health difficulties that caused a watchful eye. Ruth was the smallest at 2½ lbs and couldn't keep food down and Evelyn had kidney problems and was also very small. I didn't have any problems. I probably took all the nourishment that was provided when we were in residence in mother.

After two or three years, a special elite medical team came to observe us. Multiple births were still quite a mystery and a marvel. The dignitaries would study our behaviors, skills, abilities and, I suppose, abnormalities. We surprised them after mother had dressed us with the best we had and laid out toys to play with; the trio was all ready for the visitors, mother thought. We didn't want to play with the toys and going outdoors seemed to be a better idea. As a matter of fact, going to the fresh cultivated garden would be just fine. We completed our task by lining up a dozen worms on the front steps of the house. Instead of white garments, they were black with dirt. What a mess to observe. The doctors came to the porch and mother was sad. She asked us why we did what we did. We all responded with positive words, "we dug up worms and placed them in order on the porch so dad could go fishing." I never did find out what happened to the doctors' report. All I know is that through God's faithfulness, he provided good health and necessary needs to keep our household together.

I remember having several accidents that reminded me of God's faithfulness. I ran into a corner of a cedar chest and cut my forehead. Blood was flowing all over my face. The cut was deep but mother pulled the skin together and taped it up. I could have gouged my eye out but God was faithful to spare that. Later, I fell on the ice and my head crashed on the ice. Unfortunately, my eye came in contact with a protruding piece of ice. I spent a lot of time praying and my parents did as well to save my eye. It was a scary experience but I had a lot of help at school with friends. The accident did create some damage, but God was faithful. The next accident was a foolish mistake. I'm grateful that a guardian angel was looking out for me. I had a gun blow up in my hand. The bullet hit the wall and just missed my head. I couldn't hear for several hours, but my head was in one piece and there were no additional holes in my hand. The last accident I had at this point of my life was with a car. In the Psalms we read, "He maketh me to lie down in green pastures", which is a beautiful picture of a flock of sheep grazing in a pasture. I remember running to school because I was late. I wasn't running because I love school so much, but I didn't want to be late. I took a short cut that proved to be a serious mistake. I came head-on with a car as I turned the corner. The driver didn't see me and I didn't see the car coming due to the turn in the road. I tried to get out of the way but the gravel under my feet made me fall. The person in the car slammed on his brakes. The front wheels of the car came to a screeching stop right next to my lower back. It wasn't on a green pasture nor beside quiet waters. It was on a gravel alley road with a car just about on top of me. I'm glad that I had submitted my life to the Shepherd and that I had pursued and assimilated his Word into my daily life because I know if that car had rolled over me, I would still have had His peace and He would still lead me. In His time, He provides the pasture, quiet water and leadership. He can turn a tragedy into triumph.

There was a time in my childhood that I needed encouragement and restoration. The situation would follow me into my teens and secondary education. My path was straight from a spiritual point of view. This wasn't a spiritual problem. I was in fellowship with Jesus. I found myself in a speech therapy session in grade school. When I first started to talk I had my own means of communication. There were certain words I couldn't say. I was put in a spot many times when teachers, friends or students would just simply laugh at me because the words came out wrong. I don't think the 'enemies' to my sensitivity were trying to be hurtful. They didn't know how to react. Certain words would be said many times over and over in front of me with the expectation that I would be able to repeat them. This became a deep hardship because I couldn't say them, no matter how much kindness or anxiety was put into the effort. This developed into what I call "alternative syndrome." When I couldn't say a certain word, I would substitute it with another. This worked out quite well for me, but it led into other things. When certain subjects became very difficult, I would choose alternatives. My lifestyle was ready to change for substitutes at any given moment. Sometimes it's good to change and have proper substitutes, and at other times it's better to work through the issue and make the best of it. There are certain things we can do and there are other things that others will have to do. I think during this part of history in my life, I can say that the "good shepherd restoreth my soul." I finally was able with His strength to turn around in my thinking. The path for me to follow was found. He will be my guide and comforter.

As a child and young teenager, we would spend part of our summers at a Bible conference. This was always a great time because we would experience top Christian musicians and preachers of the day. As a matter of fact, I started my Biblical resource file in my teens with what I heard in those sessions. I have thousands of topics by reliable people at my fingertips. Of course today, it would be nice to have all that information on CD's. In the early years, I would sit on the first chair of the second row in the auditorium. Those preachers became my heroes.

"He leadeth me in the paths of righteousness." I discovered that the Shepherd could meet all my directional needs. We cannot be independent of God. He guides us. I listened during the sessions, I read the speakers books, I observed their behavior and I, even at times, asked questions. It was a time of preparation. It was a time of learning. It was a time to set goals and objectives for the present and the future. I continue to reflect upon those days today.

My first experience witnessing death came when I was a child. I spent a lot of time with my Grandpa Holmes because we lived in the same house. He was a hard worker. He taught me how to swim and he liked sports. He had a stroke that paralyzed his lower left side and upper right side and his last seven years were spent in a bed. We talked about everything. We listened to the radio together and had our special programs. He was a gentle man and liked having me around. The Bible says, "Yea though I walk through the valley of the shadow of death I will fear no evil." His death didn't take us by surprise. He was ready to meet his Maker. Passing out of this life is an exit out of one life and entrance into another. In death, trials and afflictions, I will trust and not be afraid. I learned that as we enter into the valley, we look for the opening of the gates of glory and Jesus' presence. The shadows in life will come but we don't have to be afraid. His rod protects us and His staff will pull us back into the fold. Our emotional needs can be sound and solid even with bad circumstances in our presence. I felt bad and missed my grandfather but, in my childlike faith, I knew the destiny of spirit, soul and body.

The next phrase in our text, "Thou dost prepare a table before me in the presence of my enemies; thou has anointed my head with oil, my cup overflows." This tells me that God takes care of his sheep. He will provide for our physical needs. The grain and water will provide strength for the sheep and the oil will heal the wounds and hurts. He cares for our needs. The table is a table of victory as the enemy looks on.

It's unfortunate as you read this that you cannot see my mother's face when we helped bring a big St. Bernard into our small side porch. It took my sisters, some friends and me to help bring that poor creature into our porch. Of course you know that wherever the triplets traveled, the count of individuals would probably increase at least double. The dog had a nail in its foot. We found him in the school playground. We had to help him. We said a little prayer and pulled the nail out of his foot. It wasn't as bad as we thought. Then mother helped put some ointment on it. We couldn't keep the dog but did find his parents. We already had a dog that was my buddy and protector from my sisters. We slept together, ate together, played together and did a lot together. My sisters and I became the animal lovers of the neighborhood. If anyone found a hurt creature, we would be called upon to help. If there was a dead animal, we would be called on to help. We would plan a regular service for that animal and I would share from the tract that I had found. The Psalms would be read and a few comforting memories would be shared. It all became a real ritual. We truly believed that God created and loved the animals and us. I think it became a testimony for all that participated. At least, the truth of creation, life, death and compassion would be revealed.

As I leave this period of my life, I am confident when I say "Great is Thy Faithfulness." There are many unsaid words that would cover many pages that I could have shared. When he says, "Surely goodness and mercy shall follow me all the days of my life: and I will dwell in the house of the Lord forever," these words bring encouragement, exhortation and excitement to my entire life. Just think of it, the Word surely brings authority and confidence in what will happen. Goodness and mercy will not simply follow, but will pursue me. In good days and bad days, God will be actively involved with me. I'm thankful that this text was found in my childhood. As a child of God who walks in the path of the Good Shepherd, I am always at home with God. The Shepherd says "I will never leave thee, nor forsake thee." The Lord is my Shepherd and is faithful. Eternity is welcomed with His presence, and daily life is without want.

Personal Response

Add your own review

1. How does Psalms 23 apply in daily living?
2. What does alternative syndrome refer to?
3. What substitutes do you have?

I'd Rather Have Jesus

Exodus 20:3-17

The songwriter has written, "I'd rather have Jesus than silver or gold: I'd rather be His than have riches untold; I'd rather have Jesus than houses or lands, I'd rather be led by His nail-pierced hands. I'd rather have Jesus than anything this world affords today." As I have traveled to many churches, this song has become a favorite to sing. I always played or sang a medley of songs including narration. I heard this song for the first time at a Billy Graham Crusade with Bev Shea singing. I appreciated his sincerity and the deep quality of his voice. The words and melody would follow me, lead me and give me motivation.

In 1952, I graduated from grade school with my sisters. We were kept together in those years.

The teachers said to not divide the triplets; they need to stay together. Academically, we should have been divided but emotionally we were kept together. Today there are many integrated programs for learning. Special tutoring on slow subjects would have been helpful to me. With my speech difficulties and the mastering of the alternative style of thinking, those helpful aids would have been good for me. In the early years, we missed learning words with phonics. I remember memorizing words like cat and dog by pictures not by sounds. In high school, I managed to slide by, but in college I had to do 'double duty' to keep with the flow of things.

As we grew, we continued to perform following the routine in grade school. The sounds of music rehearsal for festivals, parties, and church socials were always coming from the music room. My parents began participating with the American Sunday School Union. This brought a new dimension to our musical ministry and mother story telling. Dad, of course, always played his trombone. He actually played that instrument up to his last breath of air. He died after playing in a band performance.

In those early teen years, we continued to go to the Bible Conference. We would always find some time to retreat to that place. My best friend would travel with me no matter where I would go. His name was Prince. He was a mixed collie-shepherd dog. We spent a lot of time together. He kept me safe from my sisters. My mother loved animals but my dad didn't appreciate them too much. I became concerned for my dog so I made him eat a piece of meat with the Bible text of John 3:16 in it. He certainly had a personality but not a spirit. I was alright with that as long as I knew God created him and loved and cared for all the creatures on the earth. I taught Prince some tricks and he became a real companion. He developed a tumor in his neck and we had to put him to sleep. I have tried to block that experience out of my mind because of certain events that took place. I will leave those details out of this adventure.

In my childhood and early teens, I learned to play the cornet and trombone. My parents and school personnel were my teachers. When I became old enough to travel on the bus across the city, I started instruction at the Christian Music Center. John Scripps was an accomplished trumpeter and owned the center. In those days, it was located on top of a drug store. Today, it is a leading music instrument business in the city. In high school, I enjoyed playing in the band, orchestra, pep band and small ensembles. I also belonged to the drama club and acted in several plays and musical productions. I was never any good at sports but I still tried to participate; I played Saturday basketball. I tried out for the football team. After I got my equipment and the first practice, I threw up and got sick and dropped out. I did receive a letter for being on the track team. I can say truthfully that I never came in first, but I never came in last either.

My greatest involvement was the Campus Life Club. It was originally called Youth for Christ.

It met early Friday mornings before school. I grew personally each year in that experience by taking on various responsibilities. I started as a song leader, then vice president and then president. The club was large and at times we had over one hundred in attendance. We were always the leading contender for the city-wide rallies on Saturdays. There was a lot of competition between city clubs. I formed a 'Teen Age Gospel Team' to share the gospel at the other schools and became its director and speaker. At the city-wide events, our club was always prepared and active. I was honored several times and appreciated the opportunity to glorify the Lord.

At sixteen, I began my triple torch career. I began tutoring in my home studio. I preached with my gospel team and I mentored my students. The triple torch would be kept alive for fifty years. At the same time, I developed in my leadership. I became vice president and president of our youth ministry at church. I participated in the church choir and orchestra. From a personal point of view, I have had many friends through the Bible

Club at school and church. People would talk to me in the hall way at school that I didn't really know. I was friendly and outgoing but even at the same time I was quiet and sensitive. I had my first real girlfriend at that time. We enjoyed each other and had a lot of fun together. I discovered what that first experience would be to really care for someone of the opposite sex. It was a good journey to real love.

Every four years, the local newspaper seemed to pick up highlights in our lives. It said "Triplets 17 on the 17th in 57." Our teen years were filled with activity. In those years, I never doubted God or His Word. We lived by His rules, or better said, His principles and precepts. The Ten Commandments were committed to memory and observed. Our relationship to God and community was important. If my eyes were taken off of Jesus and my submission to him, I would fail. Through God's grace, when I made mistakes I would be forgiven. The law gives us a picture of where we are and where we should go. Later in my adult years, I would put those thoughts on paper. Read and study *The Ten Commandments for my Life* and you will find them useful.

The laws are grouped into two broad categories: Man's relationship to God and his relationship to the community. "The Book of the Covenant" (Exodus 24:7) was received by Moses on Mount Sinai, orally presented, then written down and read to the people. As a teenager, I have tried to practice them. They have become the foundation of and have brought order to my life. I shall have God before me. My top focus will always be God and his will as it is recorded in his Word. I shall have a spiritual resolve for my personal life. My top focus will be to worship God in spirit and truth, refusing idolatry. I shall have respect for God's name. My top focus will be to have reverence for his name. I shall have a physical and spiritual renewal in my life. My top focus will be complete trust in him in submissive labor. I shall have good family relationships. My top focus will be to magnify in my life what I believe. I shall have value for human life. My top focus will be to minister, protect, preserve and heal. I shall have purity in my life. My top focus will be a lifelong relationship of commitment and trust with a pure heart. I shall have good stewardship in all my activities. My top focus will be placed on honesty regarding God, family and employment relationships. I shall have absolute truth in all my decisions. My top focus will be sincerity in absorbing the truth.

I shall have a covetous heart toward God. My top focus will be an attitude of surrender to God which will provide peace and contentment. I like the word "shall" because it means with determination. It is not just an obligation. It is a necessity. My will has chosen to abide in the law. It is through God's grace and Jesus Christ's accomplishment that I can pursue it. This becomes reality through the Holy Spirit's work in me when I let him work. My mother would remind us that we live in a glass house and you can see through the glass. The law reminds me what I should do and God's gracious spirit provides the enablement. My motivation during those years would be that I'd rather have Jesus than anything. I am thankful for the conscious awareness of the Holy Spirit. I have made many mistakes but he has always brought me back on the straight road.

In 1958, I graduated from High School. The newspaper would once again share the news "Graduation with a Ring to it." We were the first set of triplets to graduate from our grade school and the second set to graduate from High School. This was a special time because we graduated together even though we had different curriculums in school. It was also special because our older sister would graduate from the Grand Rapids Baptist College three-year program at the same time.

Personal Response

Add your own review

1. Have you been called into ministry?
2. What is the story in using the Ten Commandments?

How Great Thou Art

Job 23:12

The songwriter has written, "O Lord my God, when I in awesome wonder, consider all the mighty works Thy hands hath made, I see the stars, I hear the rolling thunder; Thy power throughout the universe displayed. How Great Thou Art." My studies have been a life long journey. They include thirty years divided into three sections. Each decade would bring with it a certain unrest, challenge, and adventure along with cultural, social, political, educational and religious issues. It would depend upon the situation of the day. The studies would depend upon the need of the hour. I pursued various disciplines to achieve competence in whatever I was doing to succeed in my triple career. I really never tried to go in three's for everything. It all just came without trying. The triple urge was just simply pushing me forward. In everything, God's awesomeness never decreased. It seemed to be at every turn.

The first decade kept me busy with tutoring at several music stores in every corner of the city. This made tutoring accessible to everyone. I continued the "Teen Age Gospel Team" and preached at mission churches and also was a mentor to my students. During this time, the Word of God continued to be my foundation. The 1960's took me into traditional and non-traditional curriculum. "I have treasured the Word of God" (Job 23:12). It is my fuel to live by. It is a perfect book because it comes from God. I discovered "The fear of the Lord is the beginning of wisdom and the knowledge of the Holy One is understanding" (Prov. 9:10). The supernatural one "The Great I Am" (Ex. 3:13-14) is self-existent, self-sufficient and eternal. I have spent time at Moody Bible Institute, Grand Rapids School of Bible and Music and the National Bible College.

Some of my studies were in residence and others were through correspondence. The goal was to complete a major in Biblical Studies and earn a Bachelor of Theology degree (BTh) in order to be licensed and ordained into the Gospel ministry. This would give me doctrinal understanding of the many church schools I would be consulting at. It would also prepare me for pastoral interest. I became convinced over and over again that the Bible I learned about in my childhood was genuine. It is perfect in origin (II Tim. 3:16-17). It is God breathed. It is the very Word of God not limited to human limitations. It was "produced by the Holy Ghost" (II Pet. 1:21). The Divine Genius carried it along. He moved upon, in and through human authors. The translations of God's thoughts and will to humanity is through language and inspiration. We are not permitted to judge the Bible by our experience but we must judge our experience by the Bible, the sure word (II Pet. 1:19).

My daily activities would prove to be steady and uncertain at times but "His words shall not pass away" (Matt. 24:35). They would be perfect in purpose penetrating my very spirit and soul (Heb. 4:12-13). When I would take heed, they would provide discernment and wisdom for every decision (John 14:17). He resides in us and develops wisdom. He is the very breath of air. He provides the Scripture (Eph 6:17), "The sword of the spirit which is the Word of God." All we have to do is "hide it in our hearts" and act on it (Ps. 119:11). I learned how to study. I enjoyed research. I discovered where to go and how to accomplish my goals. This decade of education became a tool to prepare me for more in-depth studies. The new curriculum I would pursue would be built upon the original courses. At the same time I moved from tutoring to Department Manager at Grinnell Brothers Music Company. Later I would be asked to join the Marshall Music Company, the state's largest music distributor of Band and Orchestra instruments, as a school representative and new school coordinator. I would also manage my own consulting service.

The 1970's challenged me for further studies. I accepted my first interim pastorate. I learned early that people are hard to work with. My boss, Jesus, was great. I've never found any fault with him. He has never failed me. He is sovereign: "The earth is the Lord's and all it contains, the world and those who dwell in it" (Ps. 24:1). He was the founder of it. He created it. He has established it and He has sustained it. What God's soul desires, he does (Job 23:13). He works all things after His will (Eph. 1:11). The Lord has made everything for its own purpose, even the wicked for the day of evil (Prov. 16:4). "Our God in the heavens, He does whatsoever He plans" (Ps. 115:3). In Psalm 19:6 it says "the Lord our God the Almighty reigns." His attributes guarantee his sovereignty. There's nothing he cannot do. There is nothing he does not know and no location he does not exist. I learned that He knows what I'm facing. He says that He'll face it with you, and He can do the job. I'm learning to say "Thy will be done" because God rules absolutely over the affairs of men. There are no accidents with God. He does whatsoever He chooses. As we live in the world, we must think like God does, "God allows us to make choices. The destinations have been made but the route is affected by our choice. God is going to get there whether through us, around us, over us, by us or in spite of us." I loved preparing sermons. I became a master at programming. I needed to learn some more about how people think. Don't misunderstand, I love people. I know the Bible but I needed to understand how the head and heart work. In the second decade, I learned that we should obtain as much knowledge as possible. We will still come up short.

After several years, I returned back to Grand Rapids. At this time I was married and had a son. Continuing education was difficult in relationship to time spent at home, work, school and study. Sometimes I would forget sleep time or fun time. Joy, my wife, was a great helpmate. Her skills in typing and making sense out of all my research papers helped me to succeed. She is also an accomplished pianist. Therefore, she accompanied me at recitals and music juror examinations. I received a sizable grant from Aquinas College. As long as I kept up the grades, I could continue with the grant. The Lord helped me do just that. Of course, I liked what I was studying. I even wrote some of my own curriculum. I received credit for English because I wrote a booklet for publication entitled "The Gospels". I became minister of music at two churches during this period of my life. They both became a place for the display of my conducting skills and the accomplishment of certain academic requirements for conducting. I was honored to conduct several community-wide musicals. During this time I was teaching, preaching and mentoring. I don't really know how I was able to keep it all together. I graduated from John Wesley College with a Bachelors of Arts degree (BA). It was very broad in liberal arts equipping me with the triple major in Religion/Bible, Music Education and Social Science. After additional studies in education and psychology at Nazareth College, a teaching institution, I was recommended for teaching certification.

I learned a lot about humanity; the biological, psychological and even spiritual aspects. I was renewed in my thinking that "No prophetic scripture can be explained by one's unaided mental powers" (II Peter 1:20). The spiritual origin of the Word necessitates spiritual understanding. A natural man cannot receive spiritual truth. The whole concept of 'Scriptural meaning' indicates that the ministries of the New Testament are "not of the letter, but of the spirit, for the letter killeth but the spirit giveth life (2 Cor. 3:6). It is the spirit that beareth witness, because the spirit is truth (I John 5:6). We can't intellectualize or bargain with God, rather by faith we understand. My first decade of studies (1960's) paved the way and gave foundation to the second decade (1970's). Not everything you learn takes permanent root; we do not have enough soil to grow that much produce, and not all the seeds that fall into your learning tray are worthy of being cultivated. I was able to accomplish my goal once again with God's help.

In the 1980's, I found myself already with a healthy habit of studying. It seemed that everywhere I traveled in life's journey I would continue in my lifelong learning process. My interest in education wouldn't be completed with BTh and BA degrees. I became a Senior Pastor of a church on Torch Lake with interest in theology, education and counseling. In this third decade, alternative, extensive and distant education became very useful for a full time busy professional person. I naturally fell into pursuing a Master of Art and Doctor of Philosophy curriculum. My church became a part of the graduate curriculum. I enjoyed independent research; after my previous years of experience, I became proficient at this method of study. Everything I did at the church became a part of my graduate field project. It was entitled "The Development of a Local Assembly." After three years of intensive course-taking and field project innovations, I was ready to defend my Biblical Christianity Applied Project. It was a great opportunity to share Biblical truth to a liberal team of examiners. The oral exam was based on scholarship and how I presented my project. It was similar to my ordination years before, except that the first examination was given by a group of ministers upon the authority of the church and the second was composed of friendly but anti-Christian professors. The Holy Spirit led in everything I said. I had confidence and boldness. I was declared a graduate with distinction. I can truthfully say, "Hold to the things that you have learned" (II Tim. 3:12-14). The foundation and solid ground is the Holy Scripture. Anyone can read the Bible, but without the Holy Spirit's guided intelligence, the information is worth little. All of my prior training in Bible College and Liberal Arts College paid off. The study of the Word of God applied to other disciplines brought confidence. The graduate-planned program was offered in the British style of independent studies. I completed the curriculum and oral examination for my doctoral field project which displayed careful scholarship and satisfactory development of pastoral skills. I was awarded the PhD degree in religion with a specialty in Biblical Christianity through the graduate school of Columbia Pacific University.

I have a broad and integrated awareness of my overall field (Bachelor's level), and a specific developed area of competence and skills (Master's level). Now I am a teacher/innovator and a creative thinker in my specialty (Doctoral level). I was designated as an international mentor in religion upon graduation. This would give me an opportunity to serve graduate students in several countries.

"How Great Thou Art" will ring in my ears as I worship Him and serve Him. My only real goal from day one was to be "approved unto God" (II Tim. 2:15). The study of the Holy Scripture is the way to satisfy God. I have learned to cut the Scriptures straight and have become adequately equipped for all good works. I have discerned that "the entrance of thy Words giveth light" (Psalm 119:30). The Bible shows us to ourselves as God-created beings. It reveals that we come from God's hand with a purpose and plan, and that sin has entered and perverted the entire race. By one man, sin entered into the world, and death by sin (Romans 5:12). The only way to believe and be convinced of the "sure word" is through coming to the way, the truth and life found in Jesus (John 14:6). My passion is to proclaim Him in all things.

The great aim of the Christian life is not simply to know a set of ethics, but that "I may know Him" (Phil. 3:10). Throughout this whole chapter, I have emphasized why I believe in the "sure word", the Holy Scripture. It has led me all the way. When we miss Jesus, we miss what God wanted us to know. Through believing in, being cleansed by, trusting in and relying upon Him, we have life. This proclamation will continue in my life. Many people think of themselves as Christians. They are part of a community, a culture, a home and an organization which is Christian in concept and character. They are Christianized but they are not vitally related to Jesus Christ. All my studies have brought me to a relationship in knowing Jesus. I am grateful that I can sing "How Great Thou Art."

Personal Response
Add your own review

1. How was my studies divided into three decades?
2. How did I choose my major classes?
3. Did I become a teacher innovator?

Standing on the Promises
2 Peter 1:19

The songwriter has written, "Standing on the promises that cannot fail, when the howling storms of doubt and fear assail, by the living Word of God I shall prevail. I'm standing on the promises of God." I live in the 'now.' I can make daily decisions through an eternal heavenly-directive way because I am encircled with God's promises. Being 'still' has started the path. Simplicity and silence will drown out the noise and lead me to God's presence. I intend to hear His voice through His Word. The Holy Spirit dwelling within makes the abundant life a reality, not merely a possibility. The ability to put faith, hope and love into action began through His Word. His Word has opened up the door to interaction. Communication with God has brought dependence and reliance. This has been demonstrated through the re-education process and behavioral change. My life's routine has centered around His promises. This will cause radical living and bring with it ridicule, but rewards will be given at the end of it all.

As I delight in his law (Scripture), I will be blessed. The promise, "Blessed is the man who walketh not in the council of the ungodly…but his delight is in the law of the Lord" has laid the foundation (Psalm 1:12). I grew up believing in the Bible. I am extremely glad that I can say that. I do not take it for granted. I have had to unlearn a few things but the primary fundamental doctrines have been planted well into my brain waves. In those early days, if someone asked me to walk across the lake, I would have believed that God could accomplish it. If you asked why I believe, the answer would simply be that someone did it in Scripture. As long as they had their eyes on Jesus, no sinking took place. This belief remains secure because my spirit, soul and body have been entrusted in faith to Jesus Christ. I have become a soldier of Jesus Christ because "Jesus loves me this I know, for the Bible tells me so."

I can rely on the promise "Blessed is the man who walketh not in the council of the ungodly… but his delight is in the law of the Lord" because the Bible is dependable. I love books. They are my tools. I use them for many different reasons. Recently, I laid an old family Bible on a stand in my study to remind me of my history as well as the Scriptures. It is a precious book to have. It was passed down to me through my grandmother (Grandma Holmes) and to her though her grandparents. It was entered according to an Act of Congress in the year 1892 in the Office of the Librarian of Congress at Washington.

Everyone has to make a decision about the Bible, "the sure word" (2 Peter 1:19). There is no escape. Either you may cherish, read, ignore, respect, dissect, study or hate it, but a decision has to be made. I began to read that old family Bible and reflected on the fact that even though the original was written centuries ago, it is pertinent for me today. The Bible repeatedly speaks in terms that involve all generations. Jesus claimed, "Heaven and earth will pass away, but my words shall not pass away" (Matthew 24:35). The prophet Isaiah said, "The grass withers, the flowers fade, but the word of our God stands forever" (Isaiah 40:8). It claims within itself to come from an all-knowing, all-powerful, personal and exclusively-existing God. You can laugh at the Bible, and you can think that it is not relevant today. You can be a skeptic, religionist, agnostic, atheist, Satanist or just a naïve person with good ethical standards, but the Bible is still for you.

As I was reading that old family Bible, I couldn't help realize the uniqueness of it. It is different, it is one of a kind, it has no equal, it is a book written over a 1,500 year span and it was written over 40 generations. It was written by more than 40 authors from every walk of life including kings, peasants, philosophers, fishermen, poets, statesmen, scholars, etc. It was written in three continents; Asia, Africa and Europe. It was written in three languages; Hebrew,

Aramaic and Greek. It covers hundreds of topics. Yet, the biblical authors spoke with harmony and continuity from Genesis to Revelation. There is one unfolding story: God's redemption of man.

There are many reasons why the Bible is important to apply to one's life. Its dependability is connected to its uniqueness, made up of the canon, bibliographical test, internal evidence, prophesies fulfilled, historical geography, archeological evidences, miracles and its transforming power. Jesus Christ has made a direct challenge to my will to trust Him. He says, "I have been standing at the door and I am constantly knocking. If anyone hears me calling him and opens the door, I will come in" (Revelation 3:20). I discovered that when I accepted Jesus Christ as my Savior and believed He died on the cross for me and that He was resurrected, through faith my life has been changed from the inside out. I am convinced that the Bible is dependable because of the divine genius who has put it together and it has fulfilled the promise of blessing.

Holy men from God spoke as they were carried along by the Holy Spirit (2 Peter 1:21). The genius of this record is through the Holy Spirit moving upon, in and through human authors. The translation of God's thoughts and will to humanity is through language and inspiration (carried along by the Holy Spirit). The Bible (66 books contained in the Old and New Testaments) has had a divine intervention. "No prophecy ever resulted from human design." (2 Peter 1:21). "We have a more sure word of prophecy" (2 Peter 1:19) in the Bible. We are not permitted to judge the Bible by our experiences but we must judge our experience by the Bible, "the sure word."

I am convinced that the Bible is dependable because of my spiritual understanding. In my life and others' lives, Scripture has fulfilled the promise of blessing.

"No prophetic scripture can be explained by one's unaided mental powers" (2 Peter 1:20). The spiritual origin of the word necessitates spiritual understanding. Natural men cannot receive spiritual truth. The whole concept of scriptural ministry indicates that the minister of the New Testament is "not of the letter, but of the spirit, for the letter killeth but the spirit giveth life" (2 Corinthians 3:6). "It is the spirit that beareth witness, because the Spirit is truth" (I John 5:6). I can't intellectualize or bargain with God; by faith I understand. The foundation and solid ground are the Holy Scriptures. Anyone can read the Bible, but without the Holy Spirit's guided intelligence the information is worth little. The study of the Word of God brings confidence. I am convinced that the Bible is dependable because of my relationship with Jesus Christ and it has fulfilled the promises of blessing. "These are written in order that you may believe that Jesus is the Christ, the anointed One, the Son of God. Through believing and cleaving to, and trusting in and relying upon him, you may have life through His name, through what He is" (John 20:31). The life is in Him, 'what He is', and not through any religious duties, however beautifully performed. It is terrifying to know that this plain word, this "testimony of Jesus," can be in a man's possession, and he can miss the God of revelation. When we miss Jesus, we miss what God wants us to know. The great aim of the Christian life is not simply to know a set of ethics, but that "I may know Him" (Philippians 3:10).

"Blessed is the man who walketh not in the council of the ungodly…but his delight is in the law" (Psalm 1:1-2). As a soldier of Jesus Christ, I have been blessed through obeying His Word. The promise has become real in my life. I think everyone will come to a point in their life where they will be convinced that the Bible is either true or it is not. My own mind and heart had to be convinced even though I was trained as a child and young adult. I appreciated my early foundation, but I had to learn, decide and discover my own answers. I was in Chicago taking special studies at the American Conservatory of Music. One evening I picked up a book dealing with many reasons why I shouldn't believe in Christianity and the Bible. I had to come to terms with following the Bible all the way, partially, or not at all. Satan tried to be deceptive in my mind and the council of the ungodly raised some questions. Amazing as it might sound, because I have delighted in the study of God's book, the Bible, it began to convince me. Many scriptures came to my mind when my soul was troubled. Jesus said, "Let not your heart be troubled, ye believe in God, believe also in me…I am the way, the truth and the life" (John 14:1,6). I threw the other book away. It really didn't have solid reasons in it. It just gave testimony of many Christians in the church that have been poor witnesses.

I was walking on the shore of Lake Michigan and looking into the starlit sky above the blue waters. The Holy Spirit had reminded me of the Bible verses that I had learned years ago. The witness of divinity and my own spirit were united. I was truly blessed. The council of the ungodly will lead you astray but His Word will bless your life. I believe in the dependability of the Scriptures. They continue to bless me in so many different ways.

Personal Response

Add your own review

1. Why do I believe in the Bible?
2. What does it mean to have the indwelling spirit?
3. What does faith, hope, and love seen in reality?

Guide Me

Colossians 3:15-18

The songwriter has written, "Guide my steps Lord Jesus and lead me in your way, I want to be like you each moment of the day. Keep me from all sin and cleanse me within. Let God's word be my power; and strengthen me each hour." This is one of the songs I composed. It speaks of my journey in following Jesus. It was written at the dinner table. After talking with the family about Jesus Christ, we all decided to confess our sins to him. We wanted to be released of anything that would stop us from walking with Him. Our desire in the family was to allow His power to lead us and keep us safe. We would follow Colossians 3:16-17, "Let the Word of Christ dwell in you richly in all wisdom, teaching and admonishing one another in Psalms, hymns and spiritual songs, singing with grace in your hearts to the Lord. And whatsoever ye do in word or deed, do all in the name of the Lord Jesus, giving thanks to God and the Father by Him."

In my life, the proclamation of the Word has found its way primarily through music. All styles have been important to me but sacred theology and sacred music go hand-in-hand. The words, "Let the word of Christ dwell in you" is the beginning of the process. People in the church and not of it would like to minimize God's Word. We can't build our lives with man-made traditions, religious rules, human philosophies or false teachers. When Christ dwells in us, it means that He has transformed us and we have experienced His grace and peace. He feels at home in our hearts. The word 'dwell' means the same as filled according to Ephesians 5:18. As a young man and now a senior citizen, I have carried a little "Pastoral Prescription" pad. I created it to give out to people whom I visit. My first prescription was written for myself. It says,

"Above all... Christ" (John 3:31). I needed to be reminded to do some spiritual daily activities. Ask to be filled by the Holy Spirit (Luke 11:13), be fruitful and grow in discipline (I Peter 2:2), confess sinfulness (I John 1:9) and be a witness (Acts 1:8). When I do these activities, I'm all set for the day. If I forget, I'll pay the price. My early music proclamation of the Word was fulfilled through tutoring. At sixteen, I played trumpet with my older sister accompanying me at the piano. Our pastor asked if I would tutor his son so he might someday glorify the Lord in this same way. With the one student came several others. I was able to give up my lawn cutting business. I had a good little business but I was ready for a change.

Tutoring became more than a financial pursuit. I loved to watch the children mature in their musicianship. I had many opportunities one-on-one to share my faith in Jesus Christ. I developed in my skills as well. To be more accessible, I had a studio in every direction in the city. I think I have worked in just about every music store in the city at some time or another in my life.

I remained firm in my Bible foundation. It continued with these words "Richly in all wisdom, teaching." I knew nourishment from God's Word was necessary. It would equip me for every good work (II Timothy 3:16-17). I was devoted to Scripture. My life was maintained through the living Word. I was dependent upon it and therefore it directed my life. I will be tutoring until God calls me home or I don't have the health to pursue it. Tutoring introduced me to all the music stores in town. The largest downtown store at the time invited me to learn the music business. Grinnell Brothers Music Company was a part of the American Music Stores, Inc. I worked in many different departments. I moved up in various positions to department manager and possibly head manager. I enjoyed keeping track of the inventory. I was organized so my job was fun, interesting and educational. I learned about all the major instrument manufacturers. For my own students I would address what instrument was the best for them and their different types of music performance. I learned public relations and how to work with people. I became manager of my own independent music education consultant service. I enjoyed education more than business, even though they were integrated into one enterprise. I started out teaching music at West Side Christian School and finished up at East Side Christian School. I had good relations with my former business associates. I provided instruments to my students through them. Several years later, I was invited by the state's largest music industry, Marshall Music Company, to become a school service representative and new school coordinator.

Over the years, I started fifty school music departments in private and public schools. I never was interested in making money. Business was lucrative because education was the central goal. I remember at one school that I created the need to have instruments. I tested the students, coordinated the teaching staff and provided the financial necessities. They bought $100,000.00

worth of instruments. As I approached the end of my career, I have been a team teacher at several schools. I helped to teach the teacher to teach. I'm not a master teacher, but enjoyed helping others to do a more proficient job. The Lord Jesus Christ was in all that activity and the providence of God was evident.

The Scripture says, "Teach and admonish one another." The word 'admonish' means to excite, advise and exhort. I'm using all these ideas in my performance opportunities. Performing has always been a nervous experience for me but always a fulfilling activity. In my childhood, we shared in many Sunday school events, school and community activities. We added instruments to our program in our early teens and more opportunities would arrive on our door steps like concerts, recitals and festivals. Young adulthood and adulthood would provide conducting experiences. I had the privilege of conducting a city-wide Christian school concert in Grand Rapids. Several hundred vocalists and instrumentalists participated. The only part I didn't like was climbing up onto the podium. It was too high and I have a fear of heights. There was also a time when I was ready to conduct the first beat and the first row of vocalists fainted. I have conducted many church-wide musicals. I think I have enjoyed the conducting more than the instrumental performance. I have formed several ensembles over the years like the Teen Age Gospel Team, The Musical Messengers and the Messengers Inc. They were all exciting adventures. One of the ensembles became the nucleus for a larger group to perform with John Peterson in his premier musicals in Grand Rapids. This was of course a great thrill. I spent two years traveling for a humanitarian organization in music and speaking. This was an exhaustive time but full of growing opportunities. I learned that my body and mind can appreciate others doing this kind of work but I was not made for it. Physically, I can't do that kind of ministry any longer but my mind remains ready for it.

The Scripture continues, "With psalms and hymns and spiritual songs." I love this verse because one of my most rewarding excitements is putting Scripture and songs together. Those medleys have become expressions of worship. The knowledge of the Bible goes hand-in-hand with worship expression. When we sing a hymn, we address the Lord. When we sing a spiritual song, we address each other. In these last few years, I have written and arranged several medleys. *The Lord's Prayer*, *Heroes of Faith* and *Songs to Live By* have been performed in several school functions.

In all the musical activities I have participated, I have always kept the phrase "sing with grace in your heart to the Lord" in mind. Singing or playing an instrument must be done because we have God's grace in our hearts. Our performance before God is perfect even if we are out of tune. He listens to the heart. It's nice if the intonation is correct. We must do our best but God knows what is best.

The text ends with "Whatsoever you do in word or deed." This refers to all we say and do should be associated with Jesus. Our conduct magnifies our Savior and Lord. I am identified with Jesus. The word 'Christian' is found in the Scripture three times. My philosophy of music and its education is centered on the "Name of Jesus." I am so thankful to God. He has provided everything I need to do to glorify Him. In the process, I was awarded a Distinguished Service Award from the Michigan Association of School Boards for my contribution to education. I was honored on Teacher Appreciation Day from the Holland S.D.A. School. I was privileged to receive the yearbook dedication from Eastside Christian School in Grand Rapids. I was appointed to the professional extension faculty of the Sherwood Music School in Chicago (A College of Music). The most meaningful tribute came from a teenager from the Algoma Christian School. She said, "I have you to thank for my musical theory skills. God has given me a talent that through the years you have picked up on and helped me discover. Thank you so much for obeying and being a humble man of God" (Ashley Marie Lyons).

Personal Response
Add your own review

1. What is my first composition in music?
2. What is my challenge in life (Col 3:16,17)?
3. How has music been a joy in my life?

In the Service of the King

Matthew 25:21

The songwriter has written "I am happy in the service of the King, I have peace and joy that nothing else can bring. Every talent I will bring, in the Service of the King." A few years ago someone asked me, why have you followed a triple career? You have been busy in ministry and education and now you include para church leadership to your already too busy schedule. My first answer was that it is hard for me to say no, but then when I see something that needs to be done and I am able to designate and motivate others to help, I just simply fall into the activity. I'm sure my life has been hard to follow at times but as the songwriter has written, "Thro' sunshine and the shadow I can sing, in

89

the service of the King." Back in my young adulthood, John 9:4 impressed upon my heart to "work for the night cometh when no man can work." Now, in my senior adulthood, I can see the truth of that Scripture. The organizational development of several para church leadership opportunities came into place while I was still serving in ministry and education. It seems each activity grew out of the former ministry. They all had to do with John 9:4. We live in a fallen world where good behavior is not always rewarded and bad behavior not always punished. Therefore, innocent people sometimes suffer. If God took suffering away whenever we asked, we would follow him for comfort and convenience not out of love and devotion. Regardless of the reasons for our suffering, Jesus has the power to help us deal with it. Each para church ministry was developed to help a personal need and give strength through the trial and offer a deeper perspective on what is happening.

As I reflected, I discovered that the para church ministries fall into a preparation period, a volunteer period and a professional period. There was a time to be molded and to understand through sensitivity and discernment, a time to add understanding to those lifestyles through involvement and a time to put it all together. Sometimes I like to look at it with the privilege to encourage, exhort and enlighten. I like people and want to serve them.

As a child, I was given little child-like jobs to do. My folks volunteered in helping the American Sunday School Union. We would go to an Hispanic neighborhood and have a Bible class. My mother was a master story teller. We always learned something new in those classes. I would make sure everyone was welcomed. I would pass out chorus sheets and probably select someone to assist me. The color of the skin didn't make any difference to me nor did the language. I made friends with ease. I was quiet but sensitive to the other kids. I would be the first to sit by them. I really wanted them to meet Jesus. We would sing "Jesus loves me, this I know" and I would tell them my favorite Bible verse, John

3:16. A summary of the Bible was shared. I am sure in those days that we did some good. I hope I'll meet some of those children in heaven. When I started to play the trumpet in my tenth year, we would travel to the mission. The Mel Trotter Mission was on Monroe Street at that time. My dad played the trombone. The two instruments were made for each other. We performed some good duets in praise to our Lord Jesus Christ. I have some of those duets on CD's. Once again, it didn't make any difference who was performing because the testimony was for Jesus.

As a teenager, I was involved with Youth for Christ Clubs. I found myself again witnessing to the loner, outcast, neglected and rejected. It seemed that those people were drawn to me. As president of our high school club, I was always friendly and invited everyone to the club. I think I developed a sensitive nature in my childhood that simply grew with me into my teens. One day I invited a young man home with me whom I met in the school yard. He was tired, dirty, hungry and without a home. My mother fed him and gave him some clothes but all of a sudden we found a gun in his pocket. Now what do we do? We had to go to the authorities. With a lot of praying and maturing, we made it through the ordeal and everything turned out alright. I would do everything over again if I had to do it again. We had a huge club at school which gave me many opportunities to help others.

When I was teaching, I was led to start an instrumental music department at an inner city school. I had a great time working with dysfunctional and messed up family situations. If I had my way, I would have adopted all of the kids. They had some real talents and abilities. Someday I may go back to the Academy and rekindle the work.

As a young adult, I started teaching at Westside Christian School opposite from the previous school I mentioned. Everything was different. I enjoyed the privilege to teach music as a proclamation of the Word. My band room became a place to jam with students. The Bible became our resource book. Music is a great outlet in becoming friends. Encouragement and exhortation have been combined to assist the students. I have welcomed them to discussion sessions. I was able to integrate Biblical truth into a personal relationship with Jesus Christ. Christianity is progressive. We have to learn to relate everything we do and think through the Scriptures. We had numerous topics to relate to.

I completed the preparation period and began to move into the volunteer period. It started with the immediate needs of our church. We had only a few teenagers so I needed to find some teenagers. The school is the best place to find them. I was an ordained minister of the gospel but I was also a certified teacher so I became a substitute teacher. Many stories could be shared in relationship to teaching, but I need to keep to the volunteer service. The substituting led into the guidance department. I was given the opportunity to come alongside of many troubled teens. This generated interest in the church. Therefore, I hit two birds with one stone; church growth in the youth department and assistance in the school guidance department. This led into my first elected position as a trustee on the school board. Working with youth brought me in contact with a chronic liar, family abuse situations, school drop-outs and drug addiction. Through God's grace, some of the youth turned to Jesus. This was an exciting time. I have many pleasant memories to reflect upon. The substituting and guidance led into the probation court endeavors. One day I walked into the county court house to support a teenage friend. When his name was called, I walked up in front of the judge with him. The judge thought I was his attorney. As a Pastor, I asked if I could say something on the boy's behalf. The judge let me talk. After I finished, the judge asked me to come to his chambers. I wondered what I did wrong. Am I in trouble? I wondered if I said something to offend him. The judge didn't request my presence but demanded it. I stood before the judge and he put his hand out to shake mine. He said that it was a pleasure to meet me and find someone who was interested enough to stand up for the teenager. He said that if I had time and a place to handle twenty youth, he would be glad to assign them to me. It was a pleasant surprise. During this time I became acquainted with the Baptist Children's Home and Family Ministries. Some other homes were opened up for care in the community as well.

I was in the court house many times. One of those times I met a young attorney. He had just received Jesus Christ in his life. He had never lost a case. He was tough but fair. He was good at doing lawyer work but very poor at personal relationships. He had been married several times and divorced. He needed mentoring so I became his biblical advisor. I assisted him in starting a new ministry in conciliation. The Northern Michigan Conciliation Service was created and established. I was appointed the founding chairman. We worked on building solid relationships with couples on the verge of divorce who needed comfort. If we follow marriage and family relationship concepts in God's Word, we will have the answers needed to be successful. I remember praying for couples right in a corner of the court house seeking a solution. The couples would respond and want to change. Then we had to deal with their counsel representatives. Most of them worked out to the favor of the couple. Meditation seminars were set up to introduce divorce problems to the church. Counseling for the family, marriage and remarriage problems all came into focus.

Let me remind you that during all these para church activities, I was a pastor, educator and graduate student. I learned to apply everything I did to the work at hand. Everything was done in an orderly way and with proficiency. Organizational abilities were a part of my thinking system. I'm grateful for the preparation time during the 1940's and 1950's, the volunteer outreach during the 1960's and 1970's and the professional encounter in the 1980's and 1990's. When I became a Pastor, I always tried to encircle myself with professionals in different disciplines. They would become my resource people. If I needed help with assurance that I'm doing and saying the right things or to give me confidence or to have someone to discuss deep matters with, they were at my fingertips. I had a theology professor to help with Satanism issues. I had a social worker to help with an overview of social-relational problems. I had an accountant to assist with money matters. I had a psychiatrist to help with mental-medical issues and I had a medical doctor to assist with any physical or internal issues. I could call on these people at any time. They were Christians and loved the Lord. The American Association of Christian Counselors has been an ongoing educational process for me too. My primary resource has been the Bible and the Holy Spirit as my counselor.

I created a pastoral support ministry. It was called the Northwest Antrim County Ministerial Association. We had twenty pastors, representing different denominational backgrounds, meeting monthly. The fellowship was built upon Biblical Christianity concepts. We all believed in Jesus Christ through faith and enjoyed discussion on secondary issues. This gave pastors an opportunity to share church or personal problems and be lifted up through prayer and counsel. I have also had fun in helping to develop a marriage check-up and pre-marital program at Calvary Church in Grand Rapids. This was built on ten sessions leading to marriage vows. Faith and spiritual evaluation, marriage equals oneness, relational survey, couple communication, listening inventory, budget accountability, God's sexuality plan, marriage covenant, any loose ends and commitment. I continue to use this method when asked to counsel pre-marital couples today.

I asked the Lord for a more challenging opportunity to serve and He took me back to the mission. In my childhood, I played special music for the men and women before they had their dinner. You never knew what would happen. Later in Chicago I counseled at the Pacific Garden Mission. This was exciting but also a dangerous experience. I met a lot of strange people but they all needed the Savior just like me. I remember returning from Moody Church at night and two prostitutes tried to pick me up and then someone tried to rob me at knife point. In the 1990's, I was asked to direct the discipleship ministry at the Kalamazoo Gospel Mission. This is an addictive deliverance center. It had an international flavor. The men represented Europe, West Africa, Trinidad, England, Mexico and our own United States. It was interesting and exciting. I would learn to deal with different cultures in addition to the situations the men were facing. Men in recovery are traveling from helplessness to powerlessness to forgiveness. Liquor will leave you breathless, drugs will leave you senseless, but Jesus Christ won't leave you regardless. This ministry took me into many amazing situations. The Holy Spirit had to be present. My book *Discipling Dynamics* was written at this time. It was a pastoral biblical response to life's daily issues. Every time we had counseling in what I called "talk therapy" sessions, we would place our confidence on God's Word and find an answer. Along with many other strategies, success would be the result. I was pleased and proud of the guys and grateful and thankful to Jesus Christ for the

Michigan State Senate Resolution No. 300 given to the mission recognizing its contribution through the Discipleship Program. I was also honored by the Louisiana Baptist University with a Doctor of Ministry degree for integrating Christianity into the organizational development of several pastoral, educational and para church leadership ministries.

Personal Response

Add your own review

1. How did the mission service start mentoring?
2. What leadership here been a blessing?
3. How has mentoring been a joy in life?

Lamb of Glory

Romans 12:1-2

The songwriter has written "Hear the story from God's Word that kings and priests and prophets heard. There would be a sacrifice and blood would flow to pay sin's price. Precious lamb of glory, love's most wondrous story, heart of God's redemption of man – worship the lamb of glory." My passion has always been to proclaim the word of God. The Lord has helped me do it through music education and worship. He has also given me opportunity through para church ministries. Now I have come to the preaching, teaching and pastoral care ministries. I am a minister of the gospel. It is a delight to share the story of Jesus and His sacrifice. He is the precious "lamb of glory." It has been my priority in life to honor and give reverence to Jesus Christ. As I have grown, I understand a little more about what is involved. As I reflect about the pastoral ministries, I have been challenged to think about what I have learned through those years.

Someone asked me, "What is a spiritual Christian?" I think the pastor must be a Biblical spiritual Christian. I use the word Biblical because I base everything I have learned on the authority of the Scriptures. I use the word spiritual because I am thinking on spiritual terms and our dedication to a godly, righteous and holy life. I use the word Christian because Jesus Christ is my Savior, Lord and the head of the church. I will explore Romans 12:1-2 in relation to my church ministries.

Three valuable lessons have been learned that have followed my entire life. I memorized Romans 12:1-2 many years ago. I have been learning new lessons from the text every day since that day. Paul writes the text through the Holy Spirit, the divine genius of the Scripture. The first eleven chapters reveal doctrine.

From chapter twelve to the end, it deals with application. I love how the text begins; it gives me encouragement and strength. It says "I beseech you." God is talking to me and telling me that he is my helper and has come along side of me. I am not alone because the "therefore" refers to things that have taken place in my life. The four times "therefore" is in Romans refer to condemnation (3:20), justification (5:1), assurance (8:1) and dedication (12:1). I am a believer. I have been redeemed through the sacrifice of the "Lamb of glory." The penalty of sin has been solved. I'm accepted through Jesus Christ and have the assurance that I am secure in Him. When the Scripture says "brethren," it means that I have a relationship with God. This relationship is based upon Christ's death, resurrection, ascension and Pentecost. This is Biblical Christianity at its core.

I remember back in my teens. Huge decisions were made in those years. Maybe that is the reason that I love working with teenagers. My gospel praise team was ministering at a youth rally. I was speaking and I came to the end of my sermon. The Holy Spirit caused a deep sense of concern and discernment. I was facing a lot of youth my own age that needed to respond to the challenge that was just delivered. I thought about my own soul. I prayed that the convicting power of the Holy Spirit would cause a stir among us.

I also prayed that this occasion might become my call to ministry. I reached into the heavens and asked if my Lord Jesus wanted this young man to minister. If this was so, I asked the Lord to send a great response to the service, not only for confession of faith and dedication decision but to show me His will. At the end of the service, I opened my eyes and twenty youth had responded to the invitation to pray and my answer was nailed in my mind in humble appreciation. It has been many years but it seems like yesterday in my heart and mind. Seven years later, in an itinerate ministry after earning a bachelor's degree in theology, I was licensed and ordained by a Bible-believing church.

I have learned three major lessons in my pastoral ministries. It would take many words to share all the things I have learned during this time. Therefore, I have taken the top three. Everything else builds upon them. Through my life on a daily basis, I have thought about the divine residence in me, the divine transformation taking place in me and the divine will at work in me. After Christ came into my heart through the faith that He gave me, He said, "present"(Romans 12:1,2) your body, mind and will to me. The word 'present' means a definite decision. It's a once-and-for-all commitment. The words "mercies of God and reasonable service" gives me the reasons that are logical for me to give my total life to Him. As I reflect on what He has done for me, giving of Himself and then giving the Holy Spirit to me, how can I not give myself to Him? The Bible says, "present your body a living sacrifice, holy, acceptable." I have to recognize the divine residence in my body. A change has taken place because now I am a new person: "....if any man be in Christ, he is a new creature" (2 Cor. 5:17). As a Christian, the Holy Spirit dwells in me, "ye are not in the flesh, but in the spirit" (Rom. 8:9).

I have a tremendous responsibility. Will Christ be magnified in my body?

After ten years in a traveling itinerate ministry, the Holy Spirit placed the desire inside me and opened the door to stay in one place. We were holding meetings at a church that didn't have a pastor. I was invited to stay on and continue the work. Our interim ministry period started. It came at a good time because my wife and I would soon be having our first child. In our first decade of ministry, we never were able to enter into personal issues and become involved with believers' problems. This would make it possible to build relationships and easier for a young family to live. In this village church, I discovered a lot of lost souls. They were unbelievers believing they were believers. The residence of the Holy Spirit was absent. This is rather shocking thing to share but it was the truth. They lost the idea that Jesus Christ is the head of the church and the church members are in a personal, committed, trusting relationship with Him. I was reminded "know ye not that your body is the temple of the

Holy Ghost which is in you, which ye have of God and ye are not your own" (I Cor. 6:19).

The pastor's first priority is always to die to self, yield to God's will and be completely dedicated to his Lord and Savior. None of these important principles were in the village church. It really doesn't make any difference if the church is small or large. I have come to the conclusion that I must recognize the residence of the Holy Spirit. The church needed a reality check. I had to get down to the basics. It started with me. Do I realize that the God I love through Jesus Christ is dwelling in my very being, and am I living that out for all to see? I imagined what it would be like to deal with every part of life with His presence in me and the church.

We know so little about God. Even when I look into the solar system, I have really seen just the fringes of God. The God that lives in me is totally and absolutely complete within Himself. Nothing can be added to or taken away from God. I cannot box Him in. Everything that makes God who He is already resides within Him. I can believe or reject

Him, but He is still God. God is not dependent on me. I am, we all are, dependent on Him. I have served in large and small churches. I hate to say it but when I failed, it was because I forgot that He resides in me. I have made mistakes but God forgives in our repentance and confession. The greater mistake is allowing Satan to use the mistake to focus on and keep me from God. The village church and I learned that we must daily recognize His divine presence.

The next part of the verse shows me how to live out the divine presence, "Be not conformed to this world but be ye transformed by the renewing of your mind." We must not only recognize the divine presence in us, but we must respond to the divine transformation. What does it mean to be Christ-centered? Is my lifestyle based upon the world's system of belief and values? Transformation is an ongoing experience. We manifest God's redemption through our redeemed nature. The world wants to control our minds but God wants to transform us from within. The Holy Spirit releases power from inside through our spirit. This takes place when I allow Jesus Christ to dominate my life through the saturation of His Word in my mind. Christianity is a process. I have learned that in everything Christ must be the focus.

In my first full-time pastorate, I learned what it means to allow the divine residence of the Holy Spirit to bring daily transformation. Jesus Christ has been the dominate means for daily alterations in my life. I had to learn to respond to the divine demands. God says "give me your body" and now He says "give me your mind." The Christian walk is hard and especially if you are a pastor. Every eye is upon you. When Jesus says to be meek, you'd better be gentle. If He says be humble, you'd better be careful when you are proud of something that the people don't take it out of context. When He says don't worry, you'd better be strong. If you sin, confess it but take into account who you are sharing it with.

At Eastport Baptist Church on Torch Lake, we settled into a period that covered almost a decade. It could have been many more years.

It was a good place to go after short interim ministries. Just about everything I did at the church took a double meaning. The church became my graduate field project in ministry. "The Development of a Local Assembly" was my research-applied Christianity project. Being transformed myself and watching others grow in their discipleship became a careful spiritual and intellectual pursuit.

Transformation involves sound doctrine. I spent a whole year preparing and teaching Bible doctrine on Wednesday evenings. The development of a theological foundation was the starting point and the end product was a "Doctrinal Digest" manual and the Biblical resource to transform us. During this time, one of my church deacons came to me. He loved the Lord and was a servant of Jesus and His church. He was not aware of all the things he accomplished in helping me, his pastor and the church community. He asked if we could meet weekly for a time of spiritual conversation. He had many friends to talk to about community events, sports, hunting and so many other things. He was longing to talk about Jesus. Romans 12:2 was one of our dialogues and we both wanted to be transformed by the renewing of our minds. Paul says, "I urge you." He is urging us to listen, to respond and accept the gift of God. What is this gift? Our discussion led to the conclusion that we can receive a new 'electro-chemical computer' (brain-mind). Long ago people thought that the mind was an invisible inner representative of self and could be understood only by looking beyond humans for an explanation. The Greeks thought that the mind was a function of the body and that behavior was a product of the mind. Today we have many views of the mind and many different areas of study that relate to the mind. The mind and philosophy involve speculation. The mind and physiology involve observation. The mind and physics involve measurement. The mind and psychology involve testing. The mind and theology involve reconstruction. We were interested in the reconstruction part. We control our brain, our thinking and our emotion.

We are directly responsible for our actions. We choose how we think and feel. Difficulties are, for the most part, self-induced, self-maintained, self-magnified and self-distorted. My friend and I discussed how we could be free from anger, depression, envy, guilt, hatred, hostility and jealousy. It all depends on what we put our faith in. Faith requires an initiation, action and commitment.

All of this takes place in our minds. Everything we do ultimately is the result of our thoughts. What kind of mind do we want? The deacon and I wanted a renewed mind. This mind is a reflection of God's love (I John 3:23-24). I have to respond to God's demands and be under-girded by love. The renewed mind is a mind of obedience to God's commands in faith and love. It is the verification that God lives in this mind by the operating of God's spirit in our life. The renewing of our 'electro-chemical computer' (mind) is possible through faith, hope and trust. Transformation involves not only sound doctrine but the development of a Biblical organizational structure in the church. This took another year of teaching and concluded with a reliable church polity manual and behavioral strategy. Today there is increased confusion not only in regard to the great fundamentals of Christian faith but the organizational structure of the church. If the church is the assembly representing Jesus Christ, it must believe in the eternal deity of Jesus Christ, is virgin birth, His sinless life, His substitutionary and atoning death, His bodily resurrection, His high priestly ministry and His sure return. The church is going to believe in the verbal inspiration, inerrancy and complete authority of the Bible. It will have a regenerate membership based upon the individual and familial covenant with God through Jesus Christ and the Holy Spirit. The constitution and by-laws will transmit the supreme lordship of Jesus Christ and obedience to His will as revealed in the Bible. Jesus Christ is the master and there is no rule but His Word. I had an outstanding time in studying, discussing, evaluating and preparing a polity manual (behavioral digest).

The third section of the text says, "That ye may prove what is that good and acceptable and perfect will of God." I have thought about the divine residence, the divine transformation and now the divine will at work in me. God is working His will in me. He is making me like His dear Son. He is shaping me into the image of Christ. His presence, His transforming process and His will can be accomplished. I have learned that each day belongs to Him. His will is that I yield my agenda for the day to Him and let Him work it as He sees best. I have to keep in mind that He has my best interest in mind. I do not have to understand what is happening. He works in mysterious ways sometimes. His will is that I understand that the mind controls the body and the will controls the mind. His prayer is mine, "thy will be done."

A third year would involve an accountability strategy based on His will being accomplished. Many times I have worked really hard in trying to do God's will. I have tried to practice different formulas of my own to make it work. I have learned to just let go of self and let God do it. He is going to have His will accomplished. He is God. He does enable me to do His will. I have found victory, strength, courage and the knowledge to do His will.

We find this in Hebrews 13:20, 21. Let me pull each emphasis out of the text. "May the God of peace" is a phrase that says authority is found in our creator/ redeemer. He is the author and dispenser of peace. We can trust our lives to Him. Peace is the result of that trust. "Blood of the eternal covenant", the blood that Christ shed on the cross, secures God's promises for those who believe. I can rest on the decision of faith to rely on God's Word. His word is power. "Brought back from the dead", Jesus is the focus of this phrase. He is life because He conquered death. Enablement is mine through the power of the resurrection. If I believe in Christ and His power, I have access to the power of God. "Our Lord Jesus" is personal. I can enjoy my life in Christ because Jesus is Lord. He is superior and He is master. The "great shepherd", Christ, accomplished all His saving work and I have no needs that He cannot meet. He is the best caregiver. God will "equip you with everything good"; He prepares me and makes me fit and He will enable me for all I have to face. God prepares us "for doing His will and may He work in us what is pleasing to Him". Under the new covenant, He provides power to do His will and reveals His will. The key is to will my will to His. His will becomes my desire. "Through Jesus Christ" shows the emphasis not on receiving but on development. Development involves true sacrifice, obedience, discipline, fellowship and trust. "To whom be glory forever and ever", Jesus Christ is the object of glory. I have been invited to participate in God's plan to bring honor to Jesus. My entire life here and hereafter is to honor, glorify, praise and worship. When God says "Amen", it means "it is and shall be so." God will keep His promises and enable me to be all He wants me to be. His purpose will be established. I have chosen to agree with Him. "Thy will be done" means that now I watch His will at work in me.

My last full-time pastoral ministry took me into the most exciting time of my life. It would involve daily change, daily central focus and daily commitment. Mars Hill Bible Church started with several hundred people. In my former experience, churches began small and grew. I grew up thinking that a large church would be between 600 to 1,000 people. This church started at 600 in attendance. As Associate Pastor, my job every Sunday was to respond to the folks that requested assistance in their spiritual life. It was a church in fellowship. Small groups were started and eventually became house churches and a part of the larger assembly. It was a praying church. The small congregational groups became the prayer warriors for each member. It was a reverent church. It was not traditional but it was transparent. People came as they were to bow before Jesus Christ the head of the church. It was a church where things happen. This church believed that if we expect great things from God and attempt great things for God, things will happen. It was a sharing church. The believers had an intense feeling of responsibility for each other and it was a worshipping church. The people came from different backgrounds but had one thing in common. They came to worship. It was a happy church. We didn't have time to be gloomy with all the transformation taking place. It was a church that drew people. Real Christianity is a love affair.

On my first day of ministry, a young man came to me; in the previous week he had accepted Jesus Christ in his life. This week he brought a friend that needed the Savior. Right there in the hallway, his friend responded to the Holy Spirit's invitation. A continuous flow of needy souls followed this first example "thy will be done." We had hundreds of counseling sessions and with those sessions came opportunity to interview graduate students that were in an internship with us. We would see God's power in action in multiple ways. One of my greatest experiences was the participation in baptizing hundreds of people on a sunny, sandy shore. I will cherish the pictures and memories of the young and old who committed their lives to Jesus and demonstrated their obedience through baptism. It was like standing on the Jordan River in the wilderness and doing God's will. In my home study on the wall, there is a beautiful plaque that says "My heart leaps for joy and I give thanks to him in song" (Psalm 28:7). It has a musical lyre on it which emphasizes my musical proclamation of the Word and gives testimony of my first counselee at the church.

I was driving on 28th Street in Grand Rapids, Michigan and the teaching pastor of the church called me on my cell phone. He asked me if I had ever worked with someone that was having a battle with Satan, demon-possessed or under direct attack. It took me by surprise but it shouldn't have because we are always facing spiritual battles. I drove into a parking lot to give full attention to him. I thought for a moment and remembered that while I served at the Kalamazoo Gospel Mission, I had many opportunities to call on the name of Jesus for deliverance and protection. I told the pastor that I could help. He then told me that he had a man on the phone that needed God's help now! I told him to tell the guy to meet me at Meijer's parking lot. I began to pray and think about what was ahead of me.

The Bible says, "be of sober spirit, be on the alert, your adversary, the devil prowls about like a roaring lion seeking someone to devour" (I Peter 5:8). Satan's prime objective is the defeat of God. The Bible says, "we have authority over the enemy, behold I give unto you power to tread on serpents and scorpions and over all the power of the enemy, and nothing shall by any means hurt you." The word 'power' should be translated to 'authority'. It says, "behold I give you authority over the power of the enemy". The Christian does not have power over Satan. He has authority over Satan. The source of our authority over Satan is rooted in God and His power.

This first encounter caused many sessions on how to win, which is God's will for us. The gift was given for appreciation in sharing how to receive the victory. We must remain committed if we are going to win. Because of Christ's victory on the cross, we have a right to evict the thoughts that come from the flesh and the devil (2 Cor. 10:4-5). We must refocus our thought life, not to win the victory, but to receive the victory that has already been won. Only if we understand our authority can our minds be renewed. We must reprogram our minds with God's Word and His Word will increase our faith. The Bible says, "watch over your heart with all diligence, for from it flows the springs of life" (Proverbs 4:23). We must fill our minds with the wonder of Christ and desire to be like him. We must have verses of Scripture ready to quote at a moment's notice. We must always be ready to combat lies with the truth of God's Word. God himself must be first in our thinking. Are we fully committed to live to the praise of God's glory?

Do not run from Him when you fail but run to Him. After many sessions in discipleship, we discovered the divine residence, the divine transformation and the divine will. The proclamation of the Word will continue as the word of Christ dwells in me and as I respond to that word. "Worship the Lamb of Glory" with me.

Personal Response

Add your own review

1. What happened in 1940's and 1950's in preparation for outreach?
2. What happened in 1960's and 1970's in volunteer outreach?
3. What happened in 1980's and 1990's in professional outreach?
4. What happened in 2000's and 2023 in leadership outreach?

Amazing Grace

The songwriter has written. "Amazing grace! How sweet the sound! Thru many dangers, toils, and snares… and grace my fears relieved in 'tis grace that brought me safe thus far, and grace will lead me home." According to God's grace, I have been redeemed and forgiven (Ephesians 1:7). "The earth shall soon dissolve like snow, the sun forbear to shine, but God, who called me here below, shall be forever mine."

The word grace in the Bible often represents that which is limitless, since it represents realities which are infinite and eternal. It is nothing less than the unlimited love of God expressing itself in measure less grace. Grace is favor and favor is grace. What is done in grace is done graciously. Grace had brought me into the new creation in Christ Jesus. To be in Christ is to be in his infinite person, power, and glory. He surrounds, he protects, he separates from all else, and he indwells the one in Him. He also supplies in himself all that a soul will ever need in time or eternity. It is a union in Christ which is deeper than any relationship the human mind has ever conceived. (John 17:20-23).

What does it mean to magnify Jesus Christ? It is discovering God's grace at work in your personal being. I am his workmanship (Ephesian 2:10). Christ is for me (grace); it is Christ in me (faith) and Christ through me (works). I will abound because God is working through his grace. When the kingdom of God is placed first, the temporal needs are included. My dominant concern is spiritual not material. It is to think correctly which means Biblically. My life has been encircled with grace. His grace is illustrated through each chapter: Wonderful Grace of Jesus, Onward Christian Soldiers, Only Trust Him, Great Is Thy Faithfulness, I'd Rather Have Jesus, How Great Thou Art, Standin On the Promises,

Guide me, In the service of the King, Lamb of Glory, Amazing Grace.

Complete your journey read "Discovering God's Favor".

Love is compassion. It is affection, loyalty and responsible. When I do His will, I glorify Him and that is his will. God was love before He created everything. We must learn to let God be God. His model for love is sacrifice. As we practice sacrifice, we manifest His love. With that passion we can endure any discord that enters our life.

Faith is confidence. It is a decision to respond to God in His way. "I will put my faith in you," Ps. 56:3. The believer is one who has received the Lord Jesus Christ by believing on Him and now has the ability to love by faith. Faith is not based on emotions or circumstances. We can endure any discord that enters our life.

Trust is commitment to truth. Jesus Christ is the way to truth. Trust is reliance and assured hope in God. "I put my trust in you" Ps. 11:1. We can endure any discord that enter our life. Learn to trust His deliverance, goodness, providence, and safety, commit self to obedience, submission and obtain strength.

Prayer is communication. It is talking to God. It is our way to love, our way to faith, our way to trust. "Hear me when I call… hear my prayer" Ps. 4:1. "Evening, morning, and at noon, will I pray, and he shall hear my voice" Ps. 55:17. Prayer involves consuming passion, secret dialogue, and a place of solitude. Prayer is the way to prevail.

Grace is confirmation to verify that God is the authority. Grace provides love, faith, and trust. God is self-sufficient, He has no needs. He provides the power to endure hardships. When discord comes and it will, he has already provided victory.

Source

Rienecker, Fritz, *A Linguistic Key To The Greek New Testament*, Zondervan Publishing House, 1976

Zodhiates, Spires, *The Hebrew-Greek Key Study Bible*, AMG Publishing, 1984

Vaughan, Curtis, *The New Testament From 26 Translation*, Zondervan publishing House 1967

Tenney, Merrill C, *John The Gospel of Belief*, Eerdmans Publishing, 1948

Gillette, John F., *Celebrate Christ*, Chapbook Press, 2021

Gillette, John F., *Triplet's Trilogy*, J.F.G Ministry Publication, 2006

Barcky, William, *The Gospel of John*, West Minister Press, 1995

Chafer, Lewis Sperry, *Grace*, Zondervan Publishing House, 1950